Life's

A Coll

MW01228636

Martin Wiles

Published by Kindle Direct Publishing and
Love Lines Publishing

Other Books by Martin Wiles

Morning Serenity

Grits, Gumbo & Going to Church

Grits & Grace & God

A Whisper in the Woods

Don't Just Live ... Really Live

Hurt, Hope, and Healing: 52 Devotions That
Will Lead to Spiritual Health

Surviving the Church: How to Emerge Alive and Well

Sign up for more info from Martin Wiles at http://
www.lovelinesfromgod.blogspot.com.

This book is dedicated to my lovely wife, Michelle,

who understands little of my poems but encourages

me to write them, nevertheless.

FOLLOW MARTIN WILES

Faccbook (personal) https://www.facebook.com/
martin.n.michelle 309 followers, 2418 friends

Facebook (Love Lines Ministry) https://www.facebook.com/groups/258494305766463 421 members

Facebook (author page) https://www.facebook.com/martinwilesgreenwoodsc 540 followers

Twitter https://twitter.com/linesfromgod 2347 followers

Pinterest https://www.pinterest.com/martinwiles 561 followers

Linkedin https://www.linkedin.com/in/martin-wiles-5a55b14a 533 connections

Instagram https://www.instagram.com/lovelinesfromgod 684 followers

Website https://lovelinesfromgod.com 108 followers, 3500 monthly visits

Monthly contributor to the Index Journal, the Times and Democrat, and the Eagle Record newspapers.

YET I WALK

I walk the deep waters—
Faith rising to the surface—
Fear treading across my breasts—
Yet I walk . . . walk . . . walk.

The waves of life crash about—
My steps falter, my soul aches—
The wind rises as a mountain crest,
Yet I walk . . . walk . . . walk.

I run hither and thither—
Charmed by delights, won by none—
I stare fitfully at what might be,
Yet I walk . . . walk . . . walk.

A hand reaches for mine—
Scarred by hate, welcomed by love—
I grasp what many turn away,
And I walk . . . walk . . . walk.

MIGHTY YOUR HAND

Mighty your hand in the heavens—
The stars twinkle your majesty,
The planets orb your destiny,
And the expanse shouts your glory.

Mighty your hand on the earth—
Crops feeding the poor,
Good winning against evil,
And the new earth emerging yet.

Mighty your hand in the body—
Organs teaming as one,
Eyes searching for beauty,
And hands grasping for neighbors.

Mighty your hand in death—
Closing the eyes you opened,
Stilling the soul that searches,
And ushering the spirit to eternal life.

FROM MY SEATED CHAIR

From my seated chair,
And tattered porch,
I watch your rays crest the pines,
Delivering warmth to the waking fields.

Birdsongs rise to meet your call
And echo across the fallow land.
What have they to sing about,
Yet they praise with loudest tones.

Creatures large and small scamper
Some to their daylight thatches—
Others to gather for their kin—
But all pause to bathe in your light.

And from my somber perch,
I wonder at it all.
What will the day deliver,
And how many will miss your beauty.

THROUGH MY WINDOW

Your pitter patter
Crept through my window
And nestled beside me—
Rocking me into another world.

I wondered at your droplets—
Each formed and fashioned
By a master Designer above—
Each sent by love's hand.

The heavens declare your glory—
Forming your shape
Where no man dwells
And where no eye peers.

Refreshing days you bring,
Nourishment for the soul,
The ground receives your wealth,
As do the spirits of all mankind.

I FIND YOU NOT

I scale the heights—
I find you not.
I plunge the depths—
You are not there.

I search the deepest sea—
Your form I find not.
I trudge the lonely desert—
Your eyes see me not.

In the crevices of despair
My depression deepens.
Friends desert me; family flees—
Loneliness my closest friend.

Then, a ray of hope—
A light from heaven's crest.
I sense your Spirit.
My soul is revived.

I TOOK YOUR HAND

I took your small hand,
And we walked the streets
Where worry never played.

I took your young hand once more,
And we strolled the alleys
Where friends turn away
And disappointment reigns.

I took your older hand
When choices were many,
When life swirled unceasingly,
And you considered the road not taken.

Now you grasp my hand
As I walk to life's edge.
You speak peace to my fears
While the light slowly fades.

WHILST THOU BLOOM

Whilst thou bloom
From morning to noon
And from midday to dusk?

Whilst thou bloom
When rain beats your petals,
When snow covers your beauty,
When winds batter your limbs?

Whilst thou bloom
When darkness seems unending,
When warm rays turn cold,
And when trampling feet arrive?

And when your season has ended—
The smell erased from your heart—
Whilst thou bloom still
For the eternal Gardener's delight?

SEASONS

Season after season passes—
A season to be born,
To open my eyes to God's beauty
And love Mother Earth.

A season to cry—
To welcome disappointment,
To embrace sorrow,
And to traipse through the valleys.

A season to laugh—
To enjoy family and friends,
To wonder at life's complexities,
And to savor the temporary.

A season to die—
To say goodbye to life,
To long for the vast unknown,
And to walk the streets of gold.

WILDFLOWER

A wildflower you were—
Roaming to and fro, here and there—
Never settling in one place long,
Blooming here, blooming there.

One touch from those who tried.
And you closed like a fist.
No one could tame you—
You bolted like an untamed mare.

Your fragrance spread to all
But settled in no one place.
Many attempted to plant you,
Yet you would have none of it.

Then He appeared—
One stronger than your nature—
One wielding more power than you—
Now, you bloom in His bed.

AGAINST THE WIND

Round yon mountain, high and bleak,
Wind against my back,
Cold affronting my face,
I traversed the winding path.

Feet plodding o'er rocks and roots,
Toes cramped against the walls,
Hands numb within the fingers,
I kept my pace against the wind.

Breath pounding within the cage,
I kept my sight between my eyes,
Knowing one slip would end
My flight against the wind.

At last, my path gave way to way,
A calm o'ertook the sky,
And I sat to contemplate
Until next I fought against the wind.

WHEN DARKNESS ROLLS IN

When darkness rolls in,
I often cannot see
God's guiding hand before me
Or his pounding feet behind.

Snow sparkling round about me,
Crystals brimming from the air,
Waves crashing beneath my steps,
Begging my soul to devour.

"Turn back," I heard one cry,
"Move ahead," said another.
And I with eyes upturned
Kept my step another day.

With hands upon the plow,
I plod across both field and flood.
No danger shall stem my grasp,
No toil shall dim my sight.

I WORRY NOW

I worry now, but not for long,
Anxious thoughts I cannot contain.
For your beauty guards my frame,
Your sovereign work lies in each crevice.

Lilacs dance across the fields,
Lilies prance in deepest valleys,
But me, I worry and fret
For what you give in abundance.

What am I but what you've made,
A piece of dust breathed with life.
Yet in you I burst with bloom—
I radiate with color and peace.

No more will worry crouch
In my emotions, mind, or will.
Faith has driven away my foes;
I am dressed in what my Father made.

NEVER TO RETURN

Flittering high then fluttering low,
Recently released to soar.
Sun glittering off arched wings,
She reaches for never-touched parts.

Her creator calls her upward;
The condemner pulls her down.
She reaches to rise above herself,
To be what she's never been.

Once set free, she refuses
To be chained by another.
Pains in the pit, pressure from without,
Nothing can stem her tidal ride.

Free and flying on the wind,
Storms can't force her hand.
She lives her life in freedom,
Never to return to what once was.

GRACE TICKS

When tears flow
Down my sodden cheeks,
Wet with frightful thoughts,
Grace ticks loudly.

When anger rises,
Taking over my feelings,
Prodding me toward revenge,
Grace ticks clearly.

When unforgiveness tempts,
Leading to saddened moods,
Taking me to forlorn places,
Grace ticks softly.

Grace ticks when it shouldn't,
When I imagine it won't.
Grace ticks in dark and light,
For its source never sleeps.

FREELY

Freely the bell tolls,
Welcoming all who would come,
Who would claim their liberty
And release their chains.

Freely the call is made
To all who will sacrifice,
Who will give their all
And follow with no look back.

What some have abused,
Others long to hold.
What some neglect,
Others die to possess.

Until the end of time,
Freedom rings loudly.
Come, all who will.
Come sit at the Master's feast.

YOU, MY ANGEL

When the dark night of the soul
Spreads over my spirit
Like a wool-laden cover,
You, my angel, rescue me.

When the winds blow strong
And howl loud with adversity
Like wolves on a frantic hunt,
You, my angel, speak softly.

And when hope has vanished
And forlorn faces shroud
Those who fight for my joy,
You, my angel, comfort me.

You, the source of my love—
The river flowing to my heart,
The warm rays of my delight—
You, my angel, my bright morning star.

WHEN I WAS YOUNG

Wind dancing through my hair,
Days reaching to eternity,
Nights no more than dreams,
When I was young again.

The wonder of creation,
The smell of fresh flowers,
All new to a wide-eyed child
when I was young again.

Sounds of a rushing stream
Came clear and loud—
Whispers from the wind too—
When I was young again.

Nothing escaped my memory—
Thoughts haunting day and night—
All to return one fine day
When I am young again.

I SEE YOUR HAND

I see your hand
In the raging stream,
In the snowy peak
And in the wooded forest.

Your hand paints every sunset
And welcomes each sunrise.
Your fingers form the raindrops
And draw every snowflake.

I see your hand
In every newborn baby,
In each growing child,
And in every child of earth.

From young to old,
In good times and bad,
Through mountains and valleys—
I see your hand.

YOUR FACE

I see your face
In a thousand fleeting moments—
The words of comfort you spoke,
The trembling hand you grasped.

And I would bring you back,
But a great divide
Separates our minds and souls,
Taking you where I cannot come.

I keep your face before me—
Bottled in my memory,
Framed like a picture—
Lest I forget your place in my heart.

In days of long ago,
In the recesses of silence,
I see your face once more
And remember what once was.

A CROOK IN THE ROAD

The bend lay just ahead—
A crook in the road.
And beyond, a way here and there,
That took one hither and thither.

I walked to the crossed way
And paused to reflect.
Should I follow one or the other—
What changes might it bring?

Clouds hung heavily one way—
A portent of storms to come.
Rays of warmth shone on the other,
Offering peace to travelers.

An easy way beckoned to the left—
A hard way called from the next.
I stood for long at the crook,
But never chose one or the other.

ONCE AGAIN, I WAKE

Once again, I wake
And breathe the morning air.
Your glory surrounds me,
And at your beauty, I stare.

Bird songs fill the morn',
Calls from above and below.
Clouds run from here to there,
Where they go, I shall never know.

All creatures great and small
Sing their praise to your might—
Some with great voice, some not—
All thankful to be 'mid the fight.

Soon, night will descend—
All will tell the day goodbye—
Morning will break soon enough
Under your careful watchful eye.

I FELT THE BLOW

I felt the fateful blow
But not the painful hand.
I knew the heavy hurt
And walked among the shifting sand.

I walked alone into the night
While others joined their stands.
Would no one join my ranks,
Would no one be my fan?

The nights came and went—
Dragging like a slugged net—
The days passed like morning fog,
I thought, "What the use," but yet.

But hope finally arrived—
Birthed from a place deep inside—
A warm touch not seen,
A gentile voice that did not chide.

WHERE RAN MY HOPE

Where ran my hope?
Where hid my faith?
What lightened my childhood
And greeted each day with joy?

In the valley of sorrow, I roam,
Behind the veil of grief, I hide.
No hand takes my hand.
Even my best friend has fled.

But a voice hides within—
One who speaks peace in pain,
One who offers joy for tears—
And I listen with anticipation.

A hidden strength prods me on,
Taking me to mountain meadows.
There, a feast has been prepared—
Still waters for a troubled soul.

YOU HELD OUR HAND

Through the darkest valley,
You held our hand,
And when we scaled life's cliffs,
You helped us stand.

When storms raged about us—
When we could not see our way—
Your arms encompassed us,
Holding us safely through the day.

As we grew from young to old,
We followed in your steps;
Never did you lead us astray,
But untangled our thorny webs.

Our faith in you has grown—
Our every need you have met—
We welcome you into our soul,
Your love becomes our safety net.

I HEARD YOUR CALL

I heard your call,
But I came not.
The pleasures were too great,
I knew not they would rot.

You called yet again—
My mind was far away,
Turned by another star,
Too busy for your array.

Your glory I could not welcome—
Grace was beyond my grasp.
I slithered far from you,
Hiding among the rocks like the asp.

Like a hound, you pursued me—
Never turning from my rebellion—
Your mercy finally won out—
I ran to you for completion.

DARK CLOUDS

When dark clouds descend
Like billows laced with rain,
I look upon your face,
And you take away my pain.

When the sunshine of life
Refuses to send her rays,
I run to you for comfort,
And you lighten my days.

And when my joy is full,
but the peace still doesn't come,
I cling to your good graces,
Avoiding what makes me numb.

Soon, darkness gives way to light,
Lifting my spirit and goading my soul.
Once again, your mercy wins out,
And I claim what the enemy stole.

JUSTICE HAS RUN

Justice has run away,
Leaving behind hunger and death,
Tossing out the homeless,
Freezing every warm breath.

Where are the helpers,
Those whose hands are full,
Those with more than most,
Those with power to rule?

Injustice stands on each corner—
Murder, lies, theft, abuse—
Who will stand for the helpless,
Who will love and not accuse?

From heaven, a cry descends.
Justice arrives on the clouds,
Bringing vengeance with it,
Unveiling what injustice shrouds.

I WALK THE ROAD

I walk the road
Of hope upon hope—
Not looking back at falls,
Nor fearing the coming slope.

Faith holding my hand,
Mercy gracing my steps,
I limp 'neath the weight,
I lunge through the tangled web.

Grace gives me strength,
Heaven sends her rays,
Valleys vanish from my path,
And mountains lose their gray.

And I walk the road
Of hope upon hope.
Sorrow has flown to her nest,
Grief has taken leave of her robe.

YOU SEE ME

You see me
When the darkness comes,
Overtaking my emotions,
When life has delivered only crumbs.

You see me,
Alone in the fields,
Under a cloud of endless light,
And you guard me with your shield.

And you see me
When I am invisible to others,
When I am taunted and tried,
And you comfort me like a mother.

You see me
From the present to eternity,
Guarding my every step,
Leading me through each adversity.

I STAND, YOU WALK

I stand, you walk;
I sit, you run.
I see life one way,
You see nothing to shun.

I smile, you laugh;
I weep, you cry.
You see life from the top,
I have no chance to fly.

I look back, you look ahead;
I see empty, you see full.
Many call you success,
Others call me a fool.

But I know a secret—
A tale not told to all—
The last shall be first,
And the lowly shall stand tall.

TIME

Time stands for no one—
What was is no more,
What will be is not yet—
Only one knows what's in store.

Time runs from no one—
What we grasp slips away,
What we yearn for eludes—
Only one sees the wide array.

Time falls for no man—
Marching against all odds,
Battling all enemies—
Only one rises above the gods.

Time dies for no one—
Omnipotent it rises,
Fully armed it reigns—
Only one will rule the skies.

PERFECT LOVE

Perfect love drove it away
With feet bringing love
And hands offering kindness
To all who welcomed the dove.

The eyes of death grew pale,
And the grip of pain was faint.
Love stood tall and proud,
No joy could the enemy taint.

Like a daunting soldier,
Ready for battle on any front,
Love marched faster than fear,
Determined to win the hunt.

Love walked where fear could not.
Faith lined the poppy fields
Where the blood of one fell.
Love determined never to yield.

BREAKING POINT

The breaking point arrived—
The place of no return,
The end of the chord—
I felt my stomach churn.

I stood like a weathered oak—
I would not back down,
I would not turn away—
In deep waters, I would not drown.

Fear rose on one side,
Faith mounted the other side.
I pined for an escape
But found no place to hide.

Then, a light at the end—
A ray shining with hope.
I took one, then two steps;
Faith gave me the skills to cope.

THE HANDS OF GRACE

Ice-cold fingers
Slithered along my spine.
I saw life's brevity
Pass like raveled twine.

I considered the past—
I pondered the present—
I longed for hills,
But feared the descent.

Sweet smells drew me on,
Beautiful sights ne'er beheld.
Misty eyes I could not find.
Who was it that here dwelled?

Warm fingers grabbed me,
Taking me to unknown places.
With faith, I reached out
And took his hands of grace.

LOVE BENEATH THE PAIN

The hills rise up
And praise the works of your hands.
They tower over the valley below,
And marvel over your plans.

The plains reach out
To seize your marvelous works.
Flowers dance in the sunlight,
In the darkness, creatures lurk.

Oceans toss and turn,
Moving the ebbing tides.
Sea urchins ride the waves,
Displaying their faces of pride.

Deserts hide their beauty,
Revealed only to dark and rain.
But careful eyes will see
Love beneath the pain.

TOMORROW

Sunrise over mountain peak,
Sunset over ocean deep,
Walking here, dancing there,
What pilgrim's eyes cannot keep.

Waters deep ebb and flow,
Dancing 'neath the darkened sky,
Fowls cry here and there,
None so bold as they fly.

Wonder clouds his eyes;
She ponders her thoughts.
What was will once again be,
Life's games will play the plots.

Tomorrow brings another chance,
Grace cleans the slate,
Mercy picks up the fallen,
Love wipes away the hate.

IN SECRET PLACES

He dwells in secret places
Where no eye can see,
Where light cannot reach,
But where all men are free.

He inhabits quiet moments,
Ones where silence reigns,
Ones entered through prayer,
Where mercy pulsates through veins.

In secret, he doles comfort
To the troubled soul.
In darkness, he sends light
To travel o'er the knoll.

He speaks in whispers,
Not storms or strong winds.
Earthquakes carry not his word,
But a still voice he will send.

THE STRONG TOWER

I run to the tower
That is stronger than I,
That is taller than strife
And braver than my sighs.

I climb the stone steps,
Sunken by many feet,
Stumbled over by more,
And I taste the love that is sweet.

I labor with deep breaths,
Longing for a brighter day,
Panting for a level plane,
And I yearn for blue above the gray.

Finally, I stand at the peak,
Looking beyond my sorrows,
Gazing beyond the pain,
Resting in the hope of tomorrow.

EVIL RUNS

Evil runs on every side—
Wickedness here, murder there—
Those who would taint the land,
Those who have no cares.

Sorrow raises her ugly head,
And taunts those with curved lips.
She loves to press them down—
She loves to raise her whip.

Where lies a ray of hope,
Where rests a beam of light?
And evil scampers to and fro
And frolics through the night.

Yet he who rides the clouds
Will descend with fury.
He will cast his brazen arrows.
He will overcome as surely.

SHE KNOCKED

She knocked loudly on the door,
I grasped the knob but turned away.
She knocked again,
And with trembling hands, I let her stay.

Strange bedfellows we became,
As she nestled in my arms.
I sought to shoo her afar,
Knowing she pled for my harm.

Sweat graced my brow,
Panic strolled by my side.
Though I knew I should flee,
I opened my arms wide.

Once settled into my soul,
I could not shed her hide,
I wore her night and day—
She walked the aisle by my side.

A TIME

As the shadow passes overhead—
Made known by the sun's arm—
So life comes and goes,
Failing to deliver its charm.

A time for this, a season for that—
A time for birth, a time for death,
A time to rise, a time to sleep—
But all passes as a mere breath.

And what of this Maker
Who gives to one yet takes from another—
To some, the joy of glee,
To others, the loss of a brother.

A time to laugh, a time to cry,
A time to flee, a time to stand.
What comes has already been,
We cannot grasp it with bare hands.

FALL QUICKENS HER PACE

Blooms fade from sight,
Leaves release their grip,
Brown overcomes green,
Birds escape on their long trip.

Light gives way to darkness,
Warm transforms to cool,
Dew falls heavy in the dark,
Fires long for another yule.

Frowns relinquish their grip,
Smiles overcome fear,
The rain falls in torrents,
Winds blow both far and near.

Storms roll with thunder,
Clouds hang thick in space,
One season bids another goodbye,
Fall quickens her pace.

THE BRIDGE

The bridge is long,
Traversing the troubled waters,
Perching over the foamy bed,
And I wondered if it would falter.

Step after step I took,
Creaking sounds rise to speak.
I amble on with fear,
Wondering at each squeak.

Like an unending road,
The bridge marched ahead—
The creaks, the cracks, the sounds—
But I, I kept my stead.

As I reached the end
And peered back over time,
The bridge and water became one—
No trouble, no waves, no climb.

I AM LEFT TO PONDER

I run to the hills,
But they are rough and rugged—
Too steep to climb,
Too bare for my feet to hug.

I dance to the waters,
But they are too deep to cross—
The waves crash and crawl,
And I see nothing but loss.

I slink through the valley,
But it is wide and wild—
Its beauty can't hide the pain,
Its smile is but meek and mild.

But you lounge on the hills,
You swim the mighty waters,
Your form graces the valley,
And I am left to ponder.

YOUR BREATH

Your breath is my air.
Like oxygen to fresh buds,
I take it in and out,
Sucking in the life-giving flood.

Your touch is my strength.
Like a rock beneath soil,
I hold to your courage
And walk through life's toils.

Your smile is my joy.
Like rain to a parched land,
I drink in your love
As we stroll hand in hand.

Your life is my life.
Like twine twisted thrice,
Our lives are intertwined,
We will to pay love's price.

IN THE DARK NIGHT

On the good and the evil
The sun also rises.
Grace flows to the one,
Mercy walks in its guise.

Like a dove of comfort,
The Spirit rises to aid
The lowly and the poor,
Pouring out favor like shade.

The great Shepherd leads
His sheep o'er hill and dale,
Guiding through frosty woods,
Holding their hand in the gale.

And in the dark night
When the soul has lost hope,
When the mind has plunged depths,
The Father gives strength to cope.

I RUN

I run to you;
You sprint to me.
I fall but you stand,
So, I bow on bended knee.

I wonder why;
You answer not.
I raise my shield of faith,
Giving your silence little thought.

I ponder life;
You draw me upward.
I don my belt of truth
And toss the things I hoard.

I close my eyes to sleep;
You remain and work.
I release my anxiety
From the shadows in which it lurks.

AWAKEN THE DAWN

Awaken the dawn.
Sing forth loud praises
To the one who reigns—
His banner we raise.

Spring's beauty sings
Across the valleys
And o'er the mountaintops—
We will join her gladly.

Summer's warmth seizes
The breath that cries out.
But we shout the more
Lest we enjoy the drought.

Winter bares her icy fangs
At all who love her arms.
But we her burst endure
And resist her ever charm.

I WAKE

I wake with the morning;
The darkness shrouds the land,
But the night calls sound
While the morning makes her stand.

As light extends her fingers
Like the spider in the web,
Praise arises from a new day,
Where joy flows and ebbs.

Birds call, flowers open,
And night gives way to light.
Night fears make their escape,
Relinquishing their might.

Grass grows, children laugh,
And God watches with cheer.
Love grows amid the hate,
But God always remains near.

NIGHT SOUNDS

Night sounds wake with me—
The singing bird
The calling frog—
All remind me I am free.

The first rays of light
Take the night—
Bury its secrets—
Causing worry to take flight.

Soon, the night calls return—
Bringing back anxiety,
Dragging back pain—
Causing the inward parts to churn.

But whether night or day,
You hold my hand,
And walk beside me.
I will not sway.

FOR ONE

I write for one,
I live for one,
I pine for one
Until the battle is won.

I weep for one,
I laugh for another,
I long for the other
Till the lies I uncover.

Only one will suffice,
Only one will send joy.
Peace comes not from another,
Nor in another play.

Joy comes in the morning,
But only with the one.
Not to another, I turn;
Only to the one, I run.

THE LORD'S KINDNESS

The kindness of the Lord
Scales the mountain's peak,
Walks the valley's floor,
And lies beside the weak.

How deep the Lord's mercies,
How wide his grace.
His mercy runs to all;
His grace fills every space.

His loving hand reaches the lowly
And brings down the proud.
He lifts the fallen
And covers them with his shroud.

Many will sing his praises—
Many will shout to the heavens.
He will quicken the dead;
None will his children threaten.

I AM

I am, said he.
I will be
What I have been,
For I am he.

Before the mountains,
I was on high.
Before the valleys formed,
I traversed through time.

Before birds flew high,
My Spirit rose to heights.
Before animals crawled,
I walked through the nights.

I am, I was,
And will be tomorrow.
I will walk beside you
Through joy and sorrow.

THE LOVE OF GOD

The love of God
Calms the deepest fears,
Soothes the painful wound,
And dries the falling tear.

The love of God
Climbs the highest peak,
Walks the lowest valley,
And holds up the weak.

The love of God
Reaches to the East,
Extends to the West,
And cries out to the least.

God's love is vast;
God's love is wide.
How great the love of God,
From which no one can hide.

THE STAR

The star, they saw,
Which led them to a land—
Far away in a different place—
A star forged by another hand.

A star that led them
To a child, young and fair—
a child worthy of jewels
but given what they held dear.

Long the journey, little the light,
Yet the star guided their steps
And brought them safely
To the town to which they crept.

And they marveled at the sight—
At the one born a king—
Though he held no crown or robe,
He warmed their hearts like spring.

THE SEASONS

Snow spreads her blanket,
The winds cast their spell,
Leaves layer their beauty—
In winter, all is well.

Flowers display their buds,
The earth warms her crust,
Green o'ertakes death—
Spring brings life from dust.

Days march on forever,
Night says goodbye soon,
All are wrapped in warmth—
Summer from spring is hewn.

Soon, all will change,
Fall takes what summer leaves—
But one remains the same,
To him, all seasons must cleave.

YET GOD

The rains descend,
The flood waters rise.
Hope swims far away,
Yet God sends sunny skies.

The wind howls and rages,
Beating against man and beast.
Dismay blows in like a gust,
Yet God looks on the least.

Snow piles like waves,
Ice coats living and dead.
Trials fall from the sky,
Yet God gives daily bread.

Through the dead of night,
Through the heat of day—
No matter what falls our lot
God will be our stay.

I FELT YOUR HAND

I felt your hand
Gently upon my shoulder.
"Fear not, my child.
You must be bolder."

I felt your breath
Upon my neck,
Whispering in my ear,
"Don't look at the speck."

Your booming voice
Came gently to my ears—
"Tomorrow is in my hands.
Worry not about the years."

I felt your arms
Carry me o'er rock and dale.
"Be still, my child,
I have yet to fail."

I FELT THE FALL

I felt the fall
Long before it came.
It slithered through my mind,
Yet it was not the same.

The heat grew intense—
In a moment it came—
But the coolness of your Spirit
Drove away the search for fame.

Then came another wind—
Vile and filled with hate—
Like a lion, it roared
And crept through the open gate.

I sought your peace,
I ran from the fall,
I stood on solid ground,
And your grace stood me tall.

WALKING THROUGH THE SHALLOWS

Walking through the shallows—
The wind against my back,
The waves around my legs—
I feel only the pack.

The water deepens,
My pace quickens,
And with each step,
My soul is stricken.

Grief, despair, and agony
Ride each rise of foam,
Like a rider upon a steed
And a loner away from home.

I long for the celestial city
Whose gates never close,
Whose light never dims,
Whose smell is as the rose.

I SEE YOUR FACE

I see your face
In a thousand moons,
In a plethora of stars—
The rock from which I'm hewn.

I gaze at your eyes—
The starlight holds me sway—
And I wonder at their beauty
And if I'll have my way.

Your touch is warm—
In it I am secure—
Your hand soft and tender—
No other need to procure.

Together, hand in hand,
We walk into eternity.
There our souls release
And free us from adversity.

GREATER THAN

Grass springs
From winter's dearth.
Seeds sprout
From hardened earth.

Daylight grows
And warmth touches the land.
Across the sky
Arch the signs of God's hand.

Yet amid the life,
Death stretches his arm—
Taking and maiming,
Delivering his harm.

In the heavens, God sits—
Laughing at his plans.
He sees the first and last
And knows he is greater than.

DAWN BREAKS

The dawn breaks anew—
Birdsong fills the air,
Owls hoot their woes,
Driving away the night's fears.

Light breaks the sky
Where darkness once lay,
Bringing rays of joy
To toast a new day.

In heaven, the Father smiles
Over his bright creation.
And angels dance on feather clouds,
Filling the sky with elation.

All creatures great and small
Lend ear to God's symphony—
Praising he who creates wonder,
And drives away tyranny.

A LAND BECKONS

A far-away land beckons—
Where life is free
And streets are gold
And no one knows disease.

Unswept trees line the lanes,
Growing fruit for all who dwell.
Sickness and sin make their escape
To the utter depths of hell.

Free to all, costly to One—
A haven of love divine,
A lair of joy and peace
Where no heart will pine.

All walk with lightning steps,
Sleep with angels of peace,
Live where worry doesn't dwell
And love will never cease.

THE SOUNDS

The sounds of the city
Draw me to indulge,
But I know their façade—
They will not divulge.

I long for the mountains—
For unadulterated air,
Where birds sing loud
And animals have no fear.

The hills roll long,
The valleys run deep—
All who escape there
Find peace they can keep.

And when life is o'er
And the final journey made,
I'll run to the heights
Where beauty never fades.

THE RIVER

The river flows forth,
Pounding over rock and rill,
Gliding past tree and bush,
And yet it remains still.

Seasons come and go,
But still the water lies—
Spring, summer, winter, fall—
Its calmness binds the ties.

The souls of the weary
Travel there for rest—
The banks overflow
As Satan their spirits test.

Yet the river flows still,
Giving peace to all who abide.
Its source is high above—
Nothing can stem its tide.

TWO RAINDROPS

Like two raindrops
Formed on the waiting pane,
Love and mercy meet
But of themselves, don't wane.

You are high above
Yet descend to the earth;
You were God yet man,
Come to experience our dearth.

We belong to you,
And you infiltrate our souls.
We know nothing but hate
Unless we feast on your knoll.

You give love in measure
And mercy more than most.
We sit beside the stream of both,
Drinking in our fullest dose.

A CHILD AGAIN

To be a child again,
if only for a time,
to frolic, laugh, and play
in the fields of irresponsibility.

To cuddle 'neath a mother's wing
and perch upon a father's lap,
watching the world pass by—
yet not discerning its cares.

Time was of no value,
and money a simple luxury.
Days would last forever again,
if only I were a child.

The very thought of death
was so very far away—
invincibility the shield I wore,
when I was just a child.

Worry in the eyes of a child
is an adult affair,
but now I am a man
and the child is forever gone.

A MOTHER'S HANDS

A mother's hands are gentle,
cuddling her young infant,
warning her rebel teen,
guarding her adult child.

A mother's hands show kindness,
serving her partner,
loving a neighbor,
reaching those far away.

A mother's hands are wrinkled;
time has taken its toll,
but they toil still for some
who know not mothers' hands.

ACROSS THE FIELDS

Across the fields, she walks
In fear and sad array
As morning's breath descends
And shrouds her wilting folds.

She stops to speak in vain
To buds that have no cares
And sheaves that waver not,
Then melts upon her way.

And what of life, she says,
That love would leave so soon
And take with it her heart,
Her soul, and her sanity.

Then his name she does hear,
Sung through the praying boughs
And feels the touch of warmth
That cheered her long ago.

AT PEACE

Our lives are like the rose,
Bursting forth then withering away.
They are like the wind,
Gushing about then lying calm.

But for you, my friend,
The final battle is over.
You have climbed the mountain,
You have walked the valley.

Rest now, my comrade
With all the warriors of battles past.
Lay down your sword and shield,
Put away the snorting horse called life.

Behind you is a great army—
They will fight for you.
In the sweetness of your memory,
They may conquer too.

Good-bye my friend, good-bye;
You have lived with faith.
Stand now before your Creator and God.
Receive your blessed reward.

BORN OF LOVE

A nameless face, a cry,
Eyes shouting for light,
A thrusting hand and feet,
All born of love.

A waking world,
A portrait in sorrow's womb;
Choirs from the branch
Bow to claim earth's fruit.

Lingering pains of death
Resting on the breeze;
Anguish howling in peels
For peace to take its hands.

Screaming words in the night,
Blood rushing in veins.
A sudden burst
As life sees light.

A solemn hush,
A forceful prick,
Tugging lips on still breasts,
A sucking of life from death.

I AM CONTENT

Your voice I've heard
In the praying brush,
In the glistening rods—
And I am content.

The wind speaks Your name
In its every moan,
And searches the depths
Of this sinful man.

The valley my bed
For so long this time,
But now on the peak,
My sorrow is slain.

And walking with You
In dusk's quiet scenes
Has quenched my anguish
And spawned peace of soul.

IF I COULD GO BACK

If I could go back
To a time and place
Where the pace of life
Was slower, I would.

Skies were bluer then,
Water ran clearer,
Neighbors were kinder,
And nights more peaceful.

If I could go back
To my childhood days,
When time stretched slowly
To the night, I would.

Dreams passed the dark,
Hope entered my thoughts,
Fear fled from my mind,
And worry lost her fight.

If I could go back,
I'd not trade the past
For the present day,
Nor want the future.

NATURE'S CALM

Treading 'neath the bowing branch,
Embalmed by its cover and scent,
I swill the sounds of nature,
Filling my heart with joy there lent.

The driving breeze disturbs my cloak,
Soothing a spirit torn by grief,
Bearing my thoughts to distant lands
Where all is gay and sorrows brief.

On kneeling limbs, the mumbling birds
Whispered of bliss not seen on the ground,
But found alone in heaven's realm
Where peace and love thick abound.

On this note of ecstasy
With the winged fowl, I would soon fly
To skies where visions are not myths
And where souls do not die.

There I lay in nature's calm
With fragrant dreams purging my mind
Of cares and thoughts and truthful lies
That hound my steps and lurk behind.

Martin Wiles is an author, pastor, English teacher, and freelance editor who resides in Greenwood, South Carolina. He is the administrator/assistant editor for VineWords: Devotions and More and the Managing Editor for Christian Devotions. He is the founder/editor of the internationally recognized devotion site, Love Lines from God (www.lovelinesfromgod.com). His most recent book, *Surviving the Church: How to Emerge Alive and Well*, is available on Amazon. He has also been published in numerous publications. He is the husband of one, the father of two, and the grandfather of seven.

Failure to Communicate

Proverbs 13:17

"What we have here is a failure to communicate?" Many arguments and conflicts erupt when misunderstanding what someone said to us or because someone didn't comprehend what we said to them. Good communication involves multiple factors and is necessary for healthy families, businesses, community organizations and churches.

As king, Solomon relied on messengers to bring him information about kingdom affairs. There were no cell phones, planes, cars or internet to help him stay abreast. Reliable messengers delivered the right message and didn't confuse the particulars. Misinformation can lead to unwarranted actions. We have witnessed this in our age of information by making decisions on supposedly solid findings only to discover later the information was false.

Believers have the awesome responsibility to adequately and clearly communicate Christ's love. Confronting sin in the world and in people's lives is our responsibility, but how we do it is important. There were times when Jesus sternly rebuked people, but his harshest communication was reserved for those who didn't want to hear the truth. For those sincerely interested in him and his mission, his words were kind, compassionate, encouraging and loving.

Productive communication is preceded by active listening. Jesus took time to listen to the needs of those he interacted with, and we should too. We aren't there to produce spiritual epithets arising from an "I really don't care about you" attitude but to truly show concern.

Reflection: Let the messages you communicate be sprinkled with love, kindness, concern, and empathy.

Laziness Not Allowed

We do not want you to become lazy, but to imitate those who through faith and patience inherit what has been promised. **Hebrews 6:12 NIV**

When I was growing up, laziness wasn't allowed. As a first born child, my parents were out to make me responsible. I was given chores: take out the trash, help with the dishes, make my bed, clean my room. At twelve, I was using my parents' push mower to cut neighbors' yards for a small sum. When I turned fourteen, my grandfather procured me a job as a bag boy at a local supermarket. As an added source of funds, I cleaned the church my father pastored. As soon as I graduated high school, I entered the work world and have been there ever since. There are days when I feel like being lazy—and am. Sitting around isn't my style.

My parents didn't appreciate laziness, and it appears God doesn't look favorably on it either. There is a time for rest—God demonstrated that by taking a day off when He finished the work of creation—but the norm is to work diligently through the years.

Though I've never been lazy where it concerns secular work, there have been periods I've been lazy with God's business. Those times when I just don't feel like attending church, saying my prayers, teaching a class, or monitoring the nursery. And of course, when my attitude sours it becomes increasingly difficult to share my faith. Inviting someone to follow Christ with a sour attitude and a face to match rarely is inviting.

Just as physical laziness affects my health, spiritual laziness will drag down my spiritual health. There are days when I don't feel like going to work, but I go anyway. And there will be times when Satan discourages me in God's work. I must stay the course, knowing my work for God is crucial and will be rewarded by Him.

Don't let an attitude of slothfulness steal your joy and effectiveness for God.

Prayer: God of glory and grace, when an attitude of laziness steals our effectiveness for You, redirect our minds and hands to the work before us.

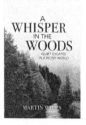

Bring on the Rain

Dear brothers and sisters, when troubles of any kind come your way, consider it an opportunity for great joy. **James 1:2**

"Into each life some rain must fall." Henry Wadsworth Longfellow.

And it did. By the bucketful. My wife and I had headed to the mountains for a few days of camping. Check in wasn't until two p.m., but the camp host said we could come anytime. Knowing the tendency of thunderstorms to crop up around noon in the mountains, we went early.

Gorgeous sunny cool weather greeted us … for one hour. No sooner had we erected the tent and put up a tarp than a gully washer marched in. My wife headed for the tent. I stood outside under the tarp. We had chosen the place for our tent based on the electrical box's location. That spot was also the low spot of the campsite.

As the water ran, it puddled several inches deep outside our tent. Soon, I heard my wife say, "We have a problem." I didn't have to ask what. Having no shovel, I used the next best thing, a hammer, to trench the water away from the tent. Then I took the broom and swept away the excess. After the rain stopped, we placed a tarp around that part of the tent to ward off any future puddles, which fortunately never came.

Campers and hikers have a saying about rain: "Rain is not a deterrent, just an inconvenience." Trials of life are similar. I wouldn't want them to stop coming, just as I wouldn't wish away the rain. Rain brings nutrients and life to God's natural order. Trials also serve important purposes. James told early believers to count is as an opportunity to have joy when they came.

Those who endure trials will receive a crown of life (James 1:12).

Trials come to believers and unbelievers alike, but believers face them with a different perspective. We suffer because we stand for Christ and have received Him as our Savior. Persecution, in whatever form it takes, is our badge of courage.

Trials also usher in God's strength (1 Peter 5:10). We have various levels of strength, but none of us can adequately face, endure, and overcome the trial without assistance from God's Spirit. Trials show up God's power in our lives. And nothing can outmatch Him.

So don't let a little rain spoil your life experience. Better things are ahead—in life and in eternity.

Prayer: Father, thank You for sustaining us through the trials of life.

Chapter One

Be Happy...The Initial Journey

Matthew 5:1-6

Since the beginning of time people have searched for the real meaning of life—happiness. Eve wasn't satisfied with the abundance of the Garden of Eden and thought she needed the forbidden fruit to complete her happiness. Some try money. Others pursue it through notoriety, power, pleasure, or immoral activities.

Experiencing the real meaning of life comes by giving up our efforts to find it and simply receiving it as God's gift. Happiness arrives through the forgiveness of our sins, which Christ paid for on Calvary. It also comes by studying and applying the practical ways he teaches to find happiness.

As Jesus begins the Sermon on the Mount, he gives a series of conditional sayings called Beatitudes which are designed to lead us to happiness. *Beatitude* isn't found in the English Bible but comes from a Latin word used by Jerome in his Latin translation.

Sadness doesn't equate with godliness and shouldn't be our constant state. Adverse circumstances may cause us to dwell temporarily "under the circumstances," but God gives us power to live above them. Nor does happiness result from changing our circumstances, but rather from trusting God to control and change them as he deems appropriate. The happiness that results from obeying the Beatitudes is not only outward, but also inward. From them we learn to be content, regardless of our circumstances.

Blessed means happy, fortunate, or blissful.

Taking a Walk

When the cool evening breezes were blowing, the man and his wife heard the Lord *God walking about in the garden. So they hid from the* Lord *God among the trees.* **Genesis 3:8 NLT**

Finally, I had reached the age of twelve—and Dad kept his promise.

The door hinges screamed like an old screen door whose spring needed a dose of oil. Dad peeked his head in to wake me, but he didn't have to call my name. I'd been awake for hours. Dad loved to hunt and eat squirrels and wanted me to, too. And this was the day I'd get my chance to do both.

Humidity hung heavily in the air, yet still offered a crisp of fall. My grandmother had always said squirrels were no good to eat until after the first frost fell. It killed the wolves (bugs), as she called them.

The river by which we'd hunt was a thirty-minute drive. Stately oaks stood like a general watching over his troops. Moss covered their branches like a quilt on a cold winter night. But I couldn't see any of this when we arrived. Daylight was at least an hour away.

We strolled through the woods. Dew decorated the limbs of the small scrub bushes, giving me a brief shower every time Dad let one flap my way. I followed Dad's flashlight beam as it scattered across the forest floor and pranced through the tree tops, looking for nests. He searched for just the right place. After all, it was my first time, and he wanted me to be successful. Finally, he found the right place.

"Sit here and wait," he said as he walked off to find his own tree.

The Genesis verse implies that God also had a habit of walking with Adam and Eve, perhaps daily. He created humanity for fellowship, so this would only be natural. Then sin entered. Satan tempted the couple, and they gave in to the one thing God had told them not to do: eat the forbidden fruit. Sin broke their intimate fellowship and brought pain.

Because God and sin don't mesh, God removed them from the garden and placed angels at its entrance to prevent their return. But he also killed an animal and placed skins over the couple's newly-discovered nakedness.

God wants the same type of relationship with everyone that he had with Adam and Eve. And when we hurt or mess up, knowing God walks with us is comforting. We've all sinned and not confessed. We get too busy in other things—good things—and focus too much on relationships with others. I could go on. You probably could, too.

The good news is that nothing in the past or the present can hinder our walk with God unless we let it. God is in the restoration business—as he proved with the first couple. No matter what we've done or are presently doing, he can cover it so the walks can continue. All we have to do is give it to him.

If something is messing up your walk with God, ask him to remove it.

Father, I want to walk with you daily. Please take away anything that prevents me from doing so.

Surviving the Church

How to Emerge Alive and Well

Martin Wiles

Some have enjoyed the best of times; others have experienced the worst.

I have seen both. People who have walked through the doors and joined up and in with smiles on their faces, only later to be devoured ... sucked up ... and then spit out like a warm glass of salt water.

My grandmother called the fish that annoyed her trash. Little fish that would not grab the hook. They would only suck the worm off. After a few times of this happening, she would say to me, "That's nothing but trash. Throw your line in a different place." She didn't want to waste the worms she had spent time cultivating or digging.

I can't remember all the names, but I can see their faces. The ones —for this or that or no reason—who sullenly walked out the same door they had excitedly walked through months or years before.

But not all were newcomers. Some comprised the pillars of the church, charter members even. They were angry over some silly thing because someone or a group didn't respond as they thought they should have. So, they threw up their hands and went somewhere else ... or nowhere.

Others got mad at preachers. After all, no pastor can please all the people all the time. Some of the discontented chose to hang around and cause further problems, while others decided to leave temporarily until the preacher did. Then they returned.

But the news isn't all bad. For each one who doesn't have good experiences in a church, many more have great experiences. Wouldn't trade their church for anything. Wouldn't think of going anywhere else, no matter how bad the preaching or singing. They hang in there through thick and thin, through the good and bad times, through the decisions they agree with and those they don't. They tolerate preachers, deacons, elders, and Sunday school teachers they don't like. They cling tenaciously to the principle that they and others can unearth common ground.

Jesus once told Peter something vital about the church: "Now I say to you that you are Peter (which means 'rock'), and upon this rock, I will build my church, and all the powers of hell will not conquer it" (Matthew 16:18 NLT).